It's Okay to Be Single!

Written by:
LAURANE SIMON

Foreword by:
PASTOR REGINA MARTIN

It's Okay to Be Single

Editing services by ChristianEditingServices.com.
Layout services by Barbara Rodriguez (yayayacreative@gmail.com).

ISBN No. 978-0-692-33555-0

PRINTED AND BOUND IN THE UNITED STATES OF AMERICA

Acknowledgments

I give full honor to God the Father, Jesus Christ the Son, and my best friend, the Holy Spirit. This book would not have been birthed had God not taken drastic measures to pull me from my own way and impart himself to me. Romans 8:28 says, "We know that in all things God works for the good of those who love him." I stand firm on that word, knowing that in all my childhood hurt and in all the mistakes and disappointments, God was working for my good.

I thank the prophetess who first released the word *author* over my life—Prophetess Regina Martin. I recall the day she spoke that word to me. I stood there looking at her and wondering, *Is she sure that "author" is what she's seeing?* I never in a million years imagined writing a book. I never had that desire, but God's plans are much greater than my own.

I must thank Prophet Warren Pitts who confirmed me as an "author" without knowledge of Prophetess Martin's word over me. Soon after, the Holy Spirit anointed me to write, and now I sit in awe, seeing my name in print as the author of this published booklet. God and the power of his spoken Word are so good.

I must also give thanks to my mother, Ismona Durogene. She has always been a walking, living, breathing example of tenacity. Thank you, Mommy, for never giving up on life, even when it wasn't easy for you or fair.

I am thankful for the great big support system I have in my family. I am stronger because of your support. Cousins answered my call to sow seeds into my dream to get this book published. I am forever thankful to Ann, Charlotte, Emmanuella, Lunie, Elainne, Cami, PK, Cathy, and Stephanie. As well, to my first friends in life: my siblings. Thank you all for the support that you give to me in every endeavor I embark upon.

To my circle of friends who immediately joined in agreement with me that I was to write my true story and went the extra mile to sow seeds of support and encouragement. I love you forever, Precious Wilcox, Nicole R. Barreau, Esq., Dr. Venessa Walker.

To my longtime friend, Christina Sears. Your stand in belief of this book gave me the fuel I needed to continue on this path. Thank you.

To my life coach, now "big sister," Lakeisha Dixon, THANK YOU! Everyone needs an encourager like you. You encouraged me when I was down, prayed for me when life got tough, laughed with me when times were funny, provided advice when I needed guidance, and offered a shoulder to lean on when my tears were streaming. Thank you for being that special individual in my life. Thank you for taking me on as a client and walking with me as a sister through every step of this book.

To my mentor and adopted mother, Rasheda Jackson, THANK YOU! You walk in a sweet spirit of love, and I can never get enough of you. Your words to me are always timely—a text, phone call, or Facebook post—as if you know what's pressing on my heart. I am forever grateful that you walked into my life and have remained beside me.

To my spiritual mother, Pastor Regina Martin, THANK YOU! God's call on your life has been a saving grace for me. Thank you for accepting his call. I encountered God through your ministry, Millennium Kingdom International Embassy. Although I was raised in church, I never really came to know God and experience his presence until that September day in 2011 at your very first revival. You are a walking example of living single in Christ. I am so thankful you saw things in me that I never knew were there. Thank you for believing in me, supporting me, and telling me the truth about myself. You have such a powerful anointing that I know will touch nations. I love you.

To my Millennium Kingdom International Embassy singles' ministry, thank you for showing up monthly for our singles' meetings. Thank you for supporting Sister Mary and me as overseers of this department. Our meetings were necessary for the vital information and experiences shared among our members. Thank you for being honest, open, and willing to allow others to benefit from your experiences.

To my men friends Lawrence, Moses, Will, and Wesley, thank you for allowing me to be a listening ear to your relationship chronicles as I traveled through this book process. Your stories confirmed to me that *It's Okay to Be Single* was a book purposed not only for women but also for men. You also confirmed that the issues women face on this journey of singleness are the same trials and challenges men face. Thank you, guys, for loving and encouraging me through the writing and publishing of this booklet.

To my girl Betty Martin Pierre, thank you for the prayers. I recall saying to God, "I pray and intercede for others, but is there anyone interceding for me?" When God showed me your face, Betty, I could do nothing but cry with gratitude. Thank you for believing in me and for always being my spiritual sister, from Parkway Middle School through adulthood. I love you to life, Boo!

This book would not read so beautifully had it not been for my editor, Jen Miller of Christian Editing Services. You are an angel sent from heaven, and we were on assignment together to get this book completed. Thank you for being so patient and gentle with me, for asking those questions, and for sharing with me your personal life testimony.

Last, but foremost, thank you Holy Spirit for speaking to my heart, "Write." This word was the beginning to this completed booklet.

Foreword

THE JOURNEY TO GREATNESS

There is a saying, "Life is like a box of chocolates. You never know what you're going to get." I also have a saying: "Cherish the people who have left an impression on your life whether small or great."

I have had the privilege of knowing this great woman of God, Laurane Simon, as my biological sister's childhood friend. Over the years I've seen Laurane overcome many trials and obstacles, but she has always sustained a smile and an encouraging, unreserved word for someone else.

The name "One Hand One Heart" depicts the makeup of Laurane's spiritual DNA. With her helping hand of love and support for others, no wonder God gave her such a name for her first Women Empowerment Seminar. Laurane has been called to greatness from her mother's womb. She is a vessel and model for such a time as this.

We each must go through our own wilderness experience, walk through our own valleys, rebuke our own mountains, but through it all we must maintain faith. I pray that as you read this book there will be a great impartation of joy as you embrace your journey through singlehood.

Remember, God is in control.

Very proud pastor,
Regina Martin

Table of Contents

Chapter 1
Blinded by the Life

I pray … that the eyes of your heart may be
enlightened … that you may know the hope to which
he has called you, the riches of his glorious inheritance.
Ephesians 1:18

I was approaching my twenty-fifth birthday with an excitement to celebrate when it became apparent to me that everyone around me was more interested in a different aspect of my life—my relationship with my boyfriend. While I was eagerly anticipating a quarter-century celebration of life, family and friends thought an engagement would also usher in the next phase of my life. In all fairness, I was thinking the same thing.

My relationship with my boyfriend appeared to be overflowing with true love. Every picture of us posted on social media exhibited my beautiful smile next to his handsome face. And his chivalry toward me further indicated he was moving closer to popping the question.

An engagement ring wasn't simply a thought on my part—my boyfriend had already placed a deposit on a ring. Conversation after conversation about wedding colors, guest list, and location swirled around me like chiffon. But God had a different plan. I was about to walk out of a relationship that appeared to have all the right ingredients for a lifelong love story … and walk into a spiritual assignment most would run from.

I was so happy as I planned the details that would make my twenty-fifth birthday party memorable—creating invitations, reserving a private dining room, selecting a special cake design and menu. There was only one problem. A gentle tugging in me had begun to pull me from the guy I thought I was madly in love with. It grew to the point where I began to have nightmares, which caused me to seriously consider that I needed to end the relationship and completely remove myself from him. I wavered in making such a drastic decision because there was really no concrete reason why I would let go of such an amazing guy. My life and future seemed to be so great with him.

I shared my feelings with my girlfriends and they thought I had gone mad. "Why do you want to leave him? He pays your bills and drops big bucks into your purse for you to have fun with on the weekends!" Some whispered, "She's stupid. I would get all his money before I left him."

Everything they said about his wealth and generosity toward me was true. He presented me with the comfortable lifestyle of a princess that promised a financially secure future. More importantly, we loved each other. By all outward signs, he would make a great husband for any woman—and I was that blessed girl.

I met him in such an innocent fashion, I didn't consider our meeting would lead to a relationship. We met through my second cousin's battle with cancer. It was the fall of 2008 and my mother was caring for her. Our cousin's health had deteriorated to the point that she could no longer chew solid food. Each Friday as I headed from Fort Lauderdale to Miami where I worked, my mother would travel with me to spend the day caring for our cousin.

My mom is a godly woman who loves and serves others. She'd clean our cousin's house and make nutritious soup to feed her while keeping her company. After work, I'd visit with our cousin before taking my mom home. It was during one of those visits that her son introduced me to his good friend—the young man who would eventually become my boyfriend.

We immediately felt a connection as friends. We laughed together and were held in rapt conversation on every subject that arose. After several weeks of just getting to know each another, he asked me if I would like to date him, exclusively. Without hesitation, I agreed.

He wined and dined me, just as a boyfriend should, and we'd talk late into the night, exchanging childhood memories and sharing current experiences and circumstances. I learned he had a little boy from a previous relationship and that he spent time with the child on weekends.

My boyfriend had a job in mental health, and though it seemed his income was well beyond his position, I didn't attempt to learn more about his job or income. This was unusual for me because I was generally one who asked a lot of questions. However, I trusted him and took him at his word about all aspects of his life. Everything about him and our relationship was like a fairytale. He was a prince who treated me like a princess.

He was a handsome, engaging, and attentive gentleman. The icing on the cake was his apparent wealth and his generosity. Frankly, he was hard to resist. He was the kind of man who opened every door and pulled out every seat as though I were royalty.

As our relationship developed, he began to help me pay my bills. He also purchased my expensive graduate books and encouraged me in every new idea I conceived. He ensured that all my emotional and financial needs were met. I had fallen hard and fast in love without a care—or a parachute. Life was really good except for that persistent tugging in me. It seemed to be pulling me toward the only area my boyfriend had not ensured I was thriving—my spiritual life.

I was raised in church and, though not a saint, I had a prayer life. When the tugging grew too strong to ignore, I had a conversation with God and asked him to reveal my boyfriend's heart to me. It was just after that simple request that I learned the power of prayer and how intimate God is in every detail of our lives. He responded just a week later.

My cell phone had begun to act up with technical difficulties. My boyfriend, being so generous, loaned me one of his many phones, intending to purchase a new one for me. That very day, after receiving the phone, God profoundly answered my prayer and drastically changed the course of my life.

The text message icon on the phone indicated a new message. Thinking the message was for me, I clicked into the history and saw that the message, along with several others, was intended for my boyfriend. As I read the first one, my jaw dropped in shock. The second one nauseated me. By the third message, I sat in total disbelief.

A plethora of emotions collided in me. I was angry that the man I loved would keep an enormous secret from me. I was disappointed in myself for not being more assertive and inquisitive early on about the details of his life. I regretted that I had allowed myself to so blindly fall into the enemy's (Satan's) trap without realizing what was happening. And I was confused by the fact that I had not put together the dangling pieces of my boyfriend's life that would have warned me something was not quite right. The truth glared sharply at me from the face of his phone. He was earning his extravagant income illegally.

Tears flowed down my face and I suddenly felt very small sitting on the side of the road in my big car, which seemed to mock me. Memories of all the times he and I had shared flashed before my eyes like a fairy tale—the impressive trips he had financed, the five-star restaurants where he had wined and dined me, the rental cars he drove and switched every other month, and the extra one-hundred dollar bills I'd find in my purse. All the caution signs had been blinking like bling in front of my face, but somehow I had been blind to them.

In answer to my simple prayer to see my boyfriend's heart, God removed the blinders and I saw the stark truth. In retrospect, I also saw the many times God had been speaking to my heart about my boyfriend, but my ears had been deaf to his voice and my heart closed to his wisdom.

The thief's purpose is to steal and kill and destroy.
My purpose is to give them a rich and satisfying life.
John 10:10 NLT

At a vulnerable time in my life—when my heart longed to be loved and cared for—the thief had slipped an ungodly man into my life. Without due thought, I had allowed the man's chivalry to sweep me off my feet and nestle me into cloud nine, primed to feel secure and loved and fall in love with him.

The very hour God opened my eyes to the truth, I wanted out of the relationship. I wanted to never see him again. My character, which had been reborn by salvation at age twelve, was opposed to his criminal lifestyle. To remain in a relationship with him would be to knowingly turn against God and against everything I believed in. I would be leading a life of deception and delinquency. Not only would my life be a lie before God and my family and friends, but also to the young girls I was mentoring. In no way did I want them to ever think it was okay to date a man who was living a fraudulent life, working as a criminal.

I didn't doubt my boyfriend had developed a true emotional love for me, but he was grossly dishonest about the life he wanted us to share. It was unfair to me and everyone in our lives.

Once I was able to compose myself, I called and confronted him about the incriminating text messages. He immediately became defensive and adamantly argued that I had not seen any such messages. He said it was impossible because he had personally removed his SIM card from the phone and inserted mine; therefore, only my messages could be retrieved.

After going back and forth in heated argument, I forwarded images of the text messages to him. He could no longer deny or argue the truth. Quietly, he said he would call me later, but I knew at that point I didn't need another call from him. I was done with him and ready to firmly close that chapter of my life.

Chapter 2
Grief, Grace, and Gratitude

These things God has revealed to us through the Spirit.
For the Spirit searches everything ...
1 Corinthians 2:10 ESV

Days later I decided it was time to go to my now ex-boyfriend's house to get my belongings. A lot had accumulated there over time. As I gathered my things, it became clear to me that I had slowly moved in with him. I hadn't realized so much of my life had been intertwined with his.

As I left his place and began the drive home, a small voice in my heart instructed me to go to Miami to visit his previous girlfriend, the mother of his son. I had no idea why, or what I would say; I just felt an inner persistence to talk with her. I had only been to her place once, the year before when I had gone with my boyfriend to pick up his son for a visit, so I could only recall the general vicinity, not the actual duplex.

It was raining heavily but the inner voice urged me on. I had been driving street to street, searching for a landmark that might jog my memory when, to my surprise, I saw her son playing in the rain. As I parked, I saw him run into a duplex. As I quickly followed, approached the door and knocked, I felt no anxiety, but neither did I have a clue why I was there or what I would say to the child's mother.

When she opened the door, her son ran into my arms and warmly embraced me. His familiarity toward me surprised her because, to her,

I was a complete stranger. I introduced myself as the girlfriend of her son's dad and she invited me in, naturally wondering if something had happened to her ex-boyfriend.

I quickly briefed her on my discovery of his illegal work and told her I had ended the relationship. And I shared that something in me had urged me to forge through the storm to talk with her. Then I inquired about her son. She responded and then took me by surprise. "Why have you only asked about our older child?"

Startled and confused, I asked, "What do you mean?" Instead of explaining, the mother stepped out of the room and a moment later returned with an eighteen-month-old boy in her arms. His eyes, nose, and facial structure screamed that he was *also* my ex-boyfriend's child. I was stunned and confused because he had never shared with me that he had second child—a mere baby!

That final roller coaster dive into truth severed all cords of feelings in me that had linked my heart to the devious man. What filled the void was gratitude to God for answering my prayer and thereby saving me from the treacherous future I was seeing in the young mother's circumstance. She explained that her ex (and mine) would not admit that the baby was his, and for that reason, he only spent time with their older son.

She and I shared a long conversation that gave us both further insight and sparked in me an altogether new and different anger—on behalf of her and her two young children. I loaded the three of them into my car and drove to his place. When we all walked in, he gasped as though a group of ghosts had suddenly materialized in his condo. He was speechless; but I wasn't. I pointed to the younger boy. "Who is this child?" He remained tongue-tied and simply stood there looking shocked.

Without confronting him further, the children's mother and I settled the boys into the living room. Then we left, forcing the man to take ownership and responsibility for the two children he had fathered.

As I drove, she cried. She had seen for herself how comfortably he was living while she struggled to support their children alone. It was all so shocking— discovering how he had further deceived me and what kind of man he truly was.

Noted poet and author Maya Angelou said, "When someone shows you who they are, believe them."

Although there were no more tears left in me over my relationship with my ex-boyfriend, I was angry and grieved that he had left all responsibility for his children on the shoulders of their mother, who was struggling to make ends meet while he lived like a king.

CȜ Ȣ

The events that followed unfolded as if I had suddenly been cast into the final season of a TV reality drama. Everyone in my life was tuned in to find out how the plot would end and what new surprises might be uncovered. I learned that his parents, his other family members, and his friends had not known he had a second child.

Despite the avalanche of truth against him, he had the gall to plead with me to reconsider my decision to end our relationship. He came by my house, sent flowers, and wrote beautiful, heartfelt love letters, but I refused to respond. It was inconceivable that I would return to a relationship built on lies or be financially supported by criminal activity.

I was only twenty-five years old and I was heartbroken and confused. Little did I know how deeply God loved me and would multiple his grace over me.

Looking back on that year of grace, age twenty-five, I did some biblical math on the number. The results profoundly impacted me. They exemplified God's intimacy in my life and how he loves me as my heavenly Father. The number five is symbolic of grace, and the number twenty is symbolic of redemption. Twenty-five—the sum of 5 x 5—would mean grace upon grace.

> *We are hard pressed on every side, but not crushed;*
> *perplexed, but not in despair; persecuted, but not*
> *abandoned;*
> *struck down, but not destroyed.*
> 2 Corinthians 4:8–9

> *"My grace is sufficient for you,*
> *for my power is made perfect in weakness."*
> 2 Corinthians 12:9

ᘓ   ᘔ

I attempted to move on with my life. I had gotten back into the groove of attending church yet my life was not producing any good fruit. God was at work, though, tilling the soil of my heart. While others had been anticipating an engagement and wanted to see me in a white dress, God wanted to see me clothed in his righteousness and hear me call him my first love. He wanted to transform me into the woman he had originally created me to be—before sin had crept in to destroy me. For this transformation, I would need to acknowledge truth, then be purified from all the toxins I had been carrying for two decades—hurt, rejection, abandonment, anger, resentment, intolerance, sexual sins. …

Chapter 3
Transformed

On September 21, 2011 my life took a drastic, near-tragic turn.

I had pulled out of my driveway and was heading east through my residential neighborhood, traveling to work. I saw children walking along the sidewalk to school and a vehicle heading west toward me. The driver had veered into my lane, heading straight for me. I pressed long on my horn but the car continued toward me—head-on. I desperately looked around for an option that would save us both but found none. I couldn't veer right because of the children, and to veer left would place me in the other lane of on-coming traffic, inviting a head-on collision of my own doing. There was no viable way out. I could only brace myself for the impact. Seconds later, BOOM! The Nissan SUV came to a crashing halt on top of my Honda Accord Coupe.

By some miracle, I was alive and still conscious. Neighbors rushed over, but instead of comforting me while waiting for an EMT as injury protocol dictates, they worked to try to pull me from the wreckage. A trail of white smoke was rising from the tangled mass of metal, threatening a greater tragedy.

A man tugged and pulled on my mangled door as I somehow managed to push from the inside. When it finally gave way, just enough for me to slide out, he helped me move to safety and laid me on the ground. Moments later, as I gasped for air, I heard the blessed sound of sirens.

As I was rushed to the nearest hospital, a burning sensation covered my body, caused by the force of the deployed air bag. My blood pressure was 175 over 110 and I had a severe headache. But miraculously, I was alive and apparently not seriously injured. Another miracle.

Sometime later I was settled in a private room in the hospital. As I waited for test results, all I could do was cry out to the Lord. I didn't understand why my life had turned in such a harsh direction, away from my hopes and dreams. I felt as though I was losing everything valuable to me. At only twenty-six, I felt as if I had been thrust into the fall season of life. People and things of value to me appeared to be withering away.

Everyone who saw my totaled vehicle uttered the same sentiment: "You should be dead!" I couldn't disagree. I knew I was the product of God's miraculous hand of protection. Recuperating in a hospital bed, the frightening claim—"You should be dead"— resounded in my head. I couldn't comprehend how or why I had escaped death virtually unscathed, but I knew deep within me that God had spared me for a reason. I was grateful and thanked him repeatedly. It was clear he had a purpose for me.

The next day, as my battered, bruised, and aching body was recovering at home, I received a text message from a pastor, inviting me to a revival service that evening. Without hesitation, I got up and began to dress. I was determined to go, though my mother was close to hysteria because I was going out so soon after a near-fatal accident, with my body in pain. Although I had thanked God for saving me so miraculously, I felt an urgency to go into his house of worship, be surrounded by his people, and again say, *Thank you, God.*

☙ ❧

The revival radically changed my life. I witnessed miraculous signs and wonders right in front of my eyes as the prophet healed the sick, released confirmation to the worried, and gave hope to the lost. That night I rededicated my life to Christ and began a journey to find true happiness and contentment in him—rather than in earthly things, such as relationships, career, money, and a certain kind of lifestyle.

As I reflected on my rededication and the belief that God had spared me for a purpose, I was reminded of Esther and her amazing journey in preparation for God's great purposes for her.

The book of Esther tells the beautiful story of an orphaned girl taken in and raised by her relative, Mordecai. He was a man of God and of faith who had reared Esther to be a noble young woman God would use beyond her wildest imagination. She would become Queen of Persia. But her marriage to the king was not God's greatest purpose for her. He would use her strategic position as queen to save her people—an entire nation—from death.

What I love about Esther's story is the purification process she went through that readied her to be selected as queen. To become purified is to follow a series of steps (a routine) that extract all toxins to bring a substance (a person in this case) back to its original form of purity.

I wanted to be made pure again before God. I wanted to know him better and follow his direction for my life, whatever that might be, but I had derailed and nearly destroyed myself. And I didn't know how I could be repaired. Though I had been raised in church, where I attended Sunday school and participated in the young adults' ministry, I had not pursued a true, intimate relationship with Christ as my Lord (Master) and Savior (Sanctifier). To be sanctified is to be made holy. God was calling me back to him to sanctify me to serve him and others in the purposes for which he had created me.

I had been viewing my life as my own rather than "bought with a price" by the blood sacrifice of God's son, Jesus, on the cross (1 Corinthians 6:20 KJV). Although I had accepted Christ as my Savior as a young teen, I had not given God a complete yes to live in obedience to him.

Instead, I had been harboring pain and anger and other toxic emotions and living according to my own reckless desires. Consequently, my spirit was infested with the toxins of sin and emotional strongholds that were preventing me from moving forward into God's great purposes for my life. The Holy Spirit of God, living in me, was grieved by those. He wanted to clean me up and clothe me in his righteousness to be a reflection of his glory.

I realized that my cleansing—my purification process—had to begin with my willingness to acknowledge and explore all the areas of my life that were stained and broken. I had to begin by speaking truth to God and myself and I had to start with my childhood.

Chapter 4
Truth

Therefore, having put away falsehood,
let each one of you speak the truth with his neighbor,
for we are members one of another.
Ephesians 4:25 ESV

The truth shall make you free.
John 8:32 KJV

I couldn't love God as I should, nor love myself as his creation, his daughter, until I had dealt honestly with my past. It had left me so deeply wounded and enraged.

Two atrocities in my childhood stole my ability to see myself as God sees me—his unique and marvelous creation, formed in his image for his glory and purposes. They also stole from me the ability to see that he wanted a close and pure Father-daughter relationship with me that would flow like a living river into my earthly relationships.

As a child, I knew who my dad was, but I never got a chance to have a relationship with him. I didn't get to know him as a dad because he had abandoned that vital role, designed by God to impart love, protection, and nurturing to me. I would often daydream about my dad; my broken heart longed for him dearly.

He had a tendency to call and make promises that he wouldn't keep. He'd tell me he was going to pick me up, but he'd never come. In one such call, he told me to get ready because he was coming to take me to meet the half-sister I'd never met. I was excited. My mother warned me he would not come, but I ignored her. I had high hopes and wanted to believe she was wrong; so I happily showered, dressed in my miniskirt and bedazzled blouse, and waited for him on the front porch. Sometime later I moved from the porch to waiting on the swing at the side of our house, where I could still watch for him. After what felt like hours, I moved to the back porch in tears of disappointment and anger.

A critical truth I didn't know as a child is this: God has reserved a place in every little girl's heart for her daddy's love and fulfilled promises. My dad's absence and empty promises left that place in my heart void and dark, lined with distrust and tender from grief and anger. That was the first atrocity.

The second one threw me into further decline. When I was nine, a neighbor molested me. I was too ashamed and scared to tell anyone, even my mother. I suffered in silence as my spirit agonized, trying to understand why that had happened to me. The harder task was trying to determine how to continue being the little girl everyone had always known me to be. My grades and behavior deteriorated, and the best I could do was mask my pain while working to push the vile memories and feelings from my thoughts.

When I grew into a young adult and began to develop relationships with young men, I lacked not only self-worth but also trust. I was not whole in spirit because those essential elements had been stolen from me. As a result, I couldn't deal honestly with the guys I dated or with myself.

When a young man, or anyone, would make a promise to me and not fulfill it, I'd instantly be thrown back into that dark hole of disappointment, abandonment, and worthlessness from my childhood. Those feelings would lead me to grief and anger, and I'd be completely done with the guy. No grace. No forgiveness. No second chances. Broken promises were too painful for me to risk allowing a second chance. Broken promises would return me to my childhood and I'd feel like that little girl again who had too often waited for her daddy to show up. I eventually grew to realize he never would.

My truth is that I gave away my virginity at age eighteen. It was the summer following my high school graduation. I was dating a guy I'd had the biggest crush on since middle school. In our senior year, he and I created many great memories.

I was looking forward to moving to Tallahassee in the fall to begin college and thought I was all grown up. I also thought I was in love with the guy and didn't think it was such a big deal to give him my sexual purity. I've since come to know through my walk with Christ that sexual purity is one of our most precious gifts from God. But as a young adult I couldn't grasp the significance of sex and certainly not the meaning of "covenant love" between a man and woman. How foolish and naive of me to think I was mature enough to embark on that journey. A sexual relationship sweeps up the mind, body, and spirit and forever changes a person.

After settling into school in Tallahassee that fall, some weekends I'd take a charter bus south to Fort Lauderdale to visit my boyfriend. My mother, who was living in our home in Fort Lauderdale, didn't have a clue I was in town just minutes from her while she thought I was miles away at school.

One such Friday evening, as I was leaving my room to go to the bus station, a framed picture of my boyfriend and me fell from my computer desk and hit the floor. The impact cracked the glass right down the middle, separating us in the picture. I didn't consider at the time that it was a sign that I needed to end the relationship. Feeding my eighteen-year-old flesh, I climbed on the charter bus and headed south to see him as usual.

We had an absolutely great weekend, but unknown to me at the time, it was the weekend I conceived a child.

Two months later, I began to experience menstrual cramps. This puzzled and concerned me because it wasn't time for my period. My cycle was like clockwork, precisely every twenty-eight days without fail, so the timing of cramps was abnormal.

The pain grew to the worst I had ever experienced. I ran from my dorm room to the restroom, but before I could get there, blood was running down my legs. My body began to shake from pain, from the quick loss of blood, and from fear. I knew something was wrong, not only by calculation of my cycle and the intensive pain but also by the color of the blood and the large clot my body released. I had no idea my body had rejected a fetus—a child. The only thing I knew was terror. I had no clue what to do afterward but go to bed. I was exhausted and temporarily anemic, so I slept. When I woke, I worked to put the experience behind me and move forward, just as I had done with every painful circumstance I had ever faced.

A few days later, the bleeding had subsided and I went to an appointment I had made months earlier for a routine Pap smear at the women's clinic. While sitting in the waiting area, I flipped through a magazine and stumbled on an article about miscarriage. As I read the signs, my heart dropped as I realized what had happened on that painful afternoon just a few days past. I didn't mention it to my doctor. I simply had the routine test, wanting to forget the ugly past. However, that evening I was overcome with tears. I felt deeply grieved by what I had carelessly allowed to happen, and I grieved over the loss of life— a tiny living treasure I had not been prepared to care for. I knew in my heart I could no longer continue in the relationship with my boyfriend, so I ended it.

The truth is, I did not value myself as God values me, so I carelessly gave away more pieces of my tattered spirit each time I blindly gave my body away sexually. The cost was not only my purity but also the loss of a life.

My sexual sin (fornication), the ensuing pregnancy, and the loss of a child had further depleted my spirit. By age eighteen, I hated the woman I saw in the mirror because of all I had lost and because of all the pain that had filled the void in my heart. The pain, emptiness, and blindness prevented me from seeing myself as Christ sees me—worth dying for, worth saving, worth God's adoption and eternal life as his princess, worth receiving "immeasurably more" than I could ask or imagine (Ephesians 3:20–21).

> **Reader:** If my truths have described yours, please ... stop now and return to God. He can restore your purity and *free you* from the bondage of sin. He can heal *all* your wounds.

Having acknowledged to God and myself the truth about my childhood and about my choices as a young woman, I was ready to be cleansed and healed as only God can. I needed to go through a purification process with him. To grow into a strong woman of God who would be ready for a mate, I needed a season of singleness to grow up under the love, protection, and instruction of my real Daddy— Abba, my Creator.

In God's love, grace, and goodness, he had to remove people and things from me to position me to become free from past pain and present expectations. This freedom would enable me to fully love him, then myself—so I could fully love others—and ready me to be loved by a mate as Christ loves. Before he would present my mate, I needed to learn what the love of Christ looks like.

Before my transformation, I hadn't realized how dark and deep were the forces of Satan to keep me imprisoned, restricted, and stagnating. I learned a very valuable lesson about the importance of speaking truth. Just as God promised in John 8:32, speaking the truth had made me free to allow his next step for me: cleansing and healing through a purification process.

Chapter 5
The Purification Process

His divine power has given us everything we need for a
godly life through our knowledge of him who called us
by his own glory and goodness.
2 Peter 1:3

In 2013, a friend (who is a nurse) suggested an herbal serum for cleansing the toxins from my physical body. I took her advice and traveled to a West Indies market where I purchased a bottle labeled Hyssop. The back of the bottle listed the herbs mixed with the hyssop to create the special blend that was to be ingested twice a day.

After taking the serum for a few days, I developed a boil on my skin— an extremely painful bump that grows larger and more painful as it fills with pus, then ruptures. After my doctor examined the boil, he prescribed an antibiotic. The boil healed, but a few months later another one appeared. I was perplexed about why my body was producing the painful sores. My mother mentioned the hyssop, and that thought was a light-bulb moment for me. I realized the herbs were doing their intended work. The boils were serving as a gathering and exit place for toxins to be released from my body.

In the same sense, before I was ready to walk into God's great purposes for me and a marriage relationship that would glorify him, I needed to rid myself of past and present wounds, sins, and strongholds that were continually producing in my spirit the toxins of hurt, anger, bitterness, resentment, insecurity, distrust, and jealousy. Similarly, my skin (the boils) had served as a temporary mask for the gathering toxins I used to conceal from others who I really was on the inside. To reveal to others all the ugliness inside me was to risk losing their love and respect. Just as a boil will eventually rupture without warning, revealing the collected toxins (the mask I wore in my relationships) would eventually burst open to reveal my true identity.

Cß   ß☯

I was determined to follow Christ through a spiritual purification process, but I wasn't sure how. A scripture in the book of Esther spoke volumes to my heart: "He speedily gave her things for purification, with such things as belonged to her" (Esther 2:9 KJV). Esther been given the tools she needed to successfully go through a purification process, but those tools already "belonged to her." She did not have to seek them out or ask for what she needed. Likewise, as 2 Peter 1:3 says, God had already placed in me everything I needed for purification "by his divine power." I simply needed to use his power in my daily life, with every thought, decision, and action.

As soon as I gave God a complete and wholehearted yes to be Lord over every area of my life, he began to deliver me from toxins in my spirit and from the sins and strongholds in my life—including fornication.

Fornication is any sexual activity between a man and woman outside the sacred covenant of marriage. The word *fornication* comes from the Greek word *porneia*, from which we get the English term *pornography*.[1] The word fornication appears thirty-five times in the King James Version Bible, warning and commanding against this sexual sin, so it's a very big deal to God. Sexual sin is not only a deadly sin against others and one's own body but also penetrates the human spirit.

The Bible warns, "Flee from sexual immorality. All other sins a person commits are outside the body, but whoever sins sexually, sins against their own body. Do you not know that your bodies are temples of the Holy Spirit, who is in you, whom you have received from God? You are not your own; you were bought at a price. Therefore honor God with your bodies" (1 Corinthians 6:18–20).

I was not married, but I had been sexually active before giving my whole heart to Christ. As I was preparing to celebrate my twenty-sixth birthday, I was sexually involved with a young man, knowing the relationship would not lead to the wedding altar. At that time, I didn't know that the intimate union of sex deeply impacts and alters the spirit. It doesn't simply connect two bodies for pleasure but also connects two spirits on a higher plane—a sacred place created and reserved by God for the holy, physical, and spiritual union of a husband and wife.

> "At the beginning of creation God 'made them male and female.' 'For this reason a man will ... be united to his wife, and the two will become one flesh' ... no longer two, but one flesh. Therefore what God has joined together, let no one separate."
>
> Mark 10:6–9

I was a child of God, uniquely created for his glory and purpose, yet I was shamelessly engaging in an activity that was *killing my spirit*. He had intended for my spirit to *thrive*. Not only was I ashamed of my sexual sins, I was ashamed that I had had more than one sexual partner. When I understood I was dishonoring and degrading God's sacred gift for marriage and the sexual purity and pleasure within that holy union and dishonoring and degrading my body and spirit that were created for his glory, I had to stop. I refused to continue living a life opposed to God and the person he had created me to be. I decided to eliminate sexual contact from my life and wait for God's blessing of marriage.

This stage in my purification process—relinquishing sexual activity—was very difficult for me. To remain true to God through celibacy, I had to be diligent to stay away from triggers—circumstances and activities that would tempt me to sin, such as certain conversations, certain media, and allowing myself to be alone with a male. I also had to be diligent to pray that the Spirit of God would keep me from sins of the flesh. Though the purification process was not easy, it was necessary in order for me to stand righteous before God and before the mate he would one day bring into my life.

Esther went through a twelve-month purification process that involved specific oils that would cleanse her and thereby position her to be selected as the king's wife, one of God's strategic steps in his plan for her. Oil is not only a cleansing agent but also a healing agent. God had been showing me that he had a specific position and purpose for my life that required that I first be healed and made pure in my spirit.

In addition to admitting my sexual sins, I had to also truthfully look at and acknowledge the other toxin-producing sins and strongholds in my life.

I was sitting in church one Sunday morning listening to a sermon on forgiveness when I began to weep. The message had immediately connected my thoughts to my dad and to the lifetime of pain and distrust I had buried deep within my heart. I couldn't stop crying as I realized I had not gotten over the fact that my dad had been an absentee dad. He had lived only fifteen minutes from me yet never followed through with his feeble attempts to be a dad to me. All I had received from him was a childhood of empty promises.

Like the mascara trailing down my cheeks with my tears, the stark blackness of two decades of unforgiveness tore my mind as I realized why I so quickly cut off every man I dated who failed to keep a promise to me. I knew on that Sunday morning I could not go from singleness to marriage carrying the weight of unforgiveness. That day at the altar, I repented and asked God to forgive me for not forgiving my dad.

Immediately, the cancerous toxins of anger, bitterness, and disappointment lifted from me. It was so tangible I could literally feel the release.

A few months later, my sister initiated a three-way call among herself, our dad, and me. He repeatedly said to me, "LoLo, I love you." For the first time in my life, I was able to receive that message from him.

Just months after that call my dad died. God had once again proven to me that his timing is impeccable. He had given me opportunity not only to forgive my dad but also to talk with him before he passed into eternity. This was my shouting moment of praise to God, my heavenly Daddy. Leading me through a purification process, he was positioning me to receive greater blessings and fulfill his greater purposes that I could not attain on my own. Though the process was painful at times, his loving hand of grace and protection were always on me. I began to see his promises fulfilled and realized he had always been at work for my good, in every circumstance.

When my heart had been broken by the man I thought I would marry, God used my brokenness to draw me to him in prayer, to open my eyes to see truth and my ears to hear his soft voice and direction.

When I was in the head-on collision that should have taken my life, God used that to prove to me that he is always in control, has a purpose for my life, and that I needed to slow down and follow him.

He used a message on forgiveness to uncover and release years of toxins from my spirit and make me new by taking me through his purification and healing process.

> *If anyone is in Christ, the new creation has come:*
> *The old has gone, the new is here!*
> 2 Corinthians 5:17

Chapter 6
Instruction

He assigned to her seven female attendants
selected from the king's palace.
Esther 2:9

Seven attendants were assigned to Esther to assist in her purification. God did the same for me. He assigned five women to my life to impart the scriptural wisdom, knowledge, insight, and direction I needed in order to be made pure of heart, to be held accountable, and to be made ready for where God would next lead me. How important it is for a young woman to have older women to provide such guidance and instruction—detailed information to achieve a desired outcome!

The story of Ruth and Boaz from the Old Testament demonstrates the significance of older women teaching and leading younger women. This story draws us to the importance of listening and following instruction.

Naomi's instruction to Ruth was for positioning Ruth so Boaz would see her characteristics, identify with them, and love her. She said to Ruth, "Wash, put on perfume, and get dressed in your best clothes. Then go down to the threshing floor, but don't let him know you are there until he has finished eating and drinking. When he lies down, note the place where he is lying. Then go and uncover his feet and lie down. He will tell you what to do" (Ruth 3:3–4).

The outcome of Naomi's instructions was love between Ruth and Boaz, which led to a powerfully purposed marriage designed by God for even greater purposes. God never joins two people for a singular purpose. He unites a man and woman as husband and wife for a multitude of kingdom purposes that will impact and alter lives for Christ and eternity. Ecclesiastes 4:9 says, "Two are better than one, because they have a good reward for their labor." This relationship may involve a husband and wife, an older person teaching a younger person, or a brother and sister partnering to accomplish something.

Naomi was older and wiser than young Ruth. Naomi had Ruth's best interest at heart—to put Ruth on a straight course to fulfill God's purposes. Ruth could choose to listen to Naomi and obey her instructions or ignore her and do things her own way. The second choice would have prevented her from fulfilling God's plans and receiving his blessings. Ruth chose to listen and obey. She said to Naomi, "I will do whatever you say" (Ruth 3:5).

In the same manner, Esther chose to position herself to hear and obey the wise instruction of her seven female attendants. As a result, she was the one chosen to serve as Queen of Persia. That critical position was designed by God not simply for marriage but also for a far greater reason: to set free an entire nation!

As a key part of my purification, I learned the critical importance of positioning myself to receive wise instruction from godly mentors. As I studied the Word of God and compared the stories of Esther and Ruth, I realized God had already placed five female attendants in my life to help push me further toward his greatness for me.

One was my overseer, my pastor and spiritual covering, Pastor Regina Martin. I chose to position my spirit to hear God's words released through her every Tuesday evening in Bible study, every Friday evening in the prayer service, and every Sunday morning in the worship service. It was Pastor Regina who had sent the text message inviting me to the revival the day after my accident.

As the heavens are higher than the earth,
so are my ways higher than your ways
and my thoughts than your thoughts.
Isaiah 55:9

During that fall season of my life, when it seemed that everything I valued was dying and falling around me like brittle leaves, God sent Pastor Regina to prepare me to enter into a new, far better and greater position in life. She not only taught me the Word of God but also lived it as a true example of a woman of God.

My life coach, Ms. Lakeisha Dixon, was another attendant assigned to me. In 2013 I heard the still, small voice of the Holy Spirit whisper to me, "One Hand One Heart Women Empowerment Seminar." I had no idea at the time what this meant or why I had received such a message. I didn't understand the magnitude of what God was orchestrating nor why those words persisted in me day after day.

One day while surfing social media, I saw an advertisement that read, "Do you have a vision that you need help to bring to life? If so, give me a call and join my vision coaching." I immediately placed the call and Ms. Dixon answered. Though we had never before spoken with each other, we chatted as if we were two long-lost girlfriends reconnected. After learning about Ms. Dixon's vision coaching, I called a close friend, Betty Pierre, and told her about it. She immediately agreed to sign up to participate in the sessions with me.

I say to you, if two of you agree on earth
about anything they ask,
it will be done for them by my Father in heaven.
Matthew 18:19 ESV

During the following weeks, Betty and I met with Ms. Dixon by phone conference for the sessions. Each meeting was electric as we entered into prayer together.

With the instruction and assistance of Ms. Dixon, on October 12, 2013, 120 women gathered in Fort Lauderdale, Florida for the first One Hand One Heart Women Empowerment Seminar. The theme was "Center of It All," purposed to empower women to live their best lives—through Jesus Christ. On that day, I gained understanding of the importance of giving God a complete and total *yes*. The women laughed and developed new friendships, and some cried as they opened their hearts to God in honesty about their lives and their need for his strength to move forward in daily life.

As I was planning the event, I heard a soft, sweet voice in my memory and knew it was the voice of the woman who would set the tone at the seminar for the Holy Spirit's work. The voice sounded familiar, and I remembered a sweet woman of God I had met during a women's conference at my church. She had hugged me and said, "Heel your way out. Because you have been faithful to God, he is ready to bless you, and because you have a sweet heart, you shall reap all your heart's desires."

That sweet, gentle voice in my memory was Pastor Rasheda Jackson's. I knew she was the one I was to ask to be the speaker for the seminar. I did some research to find her phone number and called her. I shared the vision for the seminar and asked if she would serve as the speaker. She immediately checked her calendar and agreed. When I inquired about her fee, she stopped me in my tracks and politely told me to keep my money. "I'm on assignment from God, so I won't take any money from your ministry."

When Pastor Rasheda spoke to the women, her voice was that soft, sweet sound I had heard in my spirit while planning the event. I had not shared with her the details of the message God had placed in my heart but had simply trusted him to move through the speaker according to his plan. The message she spoke, although we had not discussed it beforehand, was as if she had sat down with me during the planning stage and taken part in my thoughts! It was stunning and amazing to experience the unity of God between us. Clearly, his Spirit had united our thoughts. This was made all the more evident by the women's response to her message. They lined up at the altar, crying out to the Lord for salvation and releasing their burdens to him. I had assumed the seminar was simply to impart encouragement, but the result of God's work through Pastor Rasheda was a powerful salvation movement of the Holy Spirit.

After the seminar, I thought my purpose with Pastor Rasheda was complete, but she took me into a treasured relationship as if I were her surrogate daughter. She would call or text at the precise moments when I was discouraged or confused. She even showed up at my house on a Saturday in late 2013 as I was preparing to outline my calendar for the upcoming year and helped me discern God's direction.

Another attendant was a co-worker, Sharon Lane Jordan. The very first week we met, I nicknamed her "Sunday School" because she drove this scripture into me: "Study to shew thyself approved unto God, a workman that needeth not to be ashamed, rightly dividing the word of truth" (2 Timothy 2:15 KJV).

After I named her "Sunday School," I learned that she was serving as a Sunday school teacher in her church. She carried into every area of her life the gift of teaching God's Word, and she provided me with a firm voice of biblical direction and guidance.

The old cliché "You can't see the forest for the trees" best explains what the attendant Mrs. Jordan was to me. She had a naturally strong voice that pulled me up whenever I felt overwhelmed by life. Many times her voice helped me put life into perspective, especially when I wanted to walk away from situations in which I needed to stand strong. She saw God's calling on my life and helped me avoid feeling bombarded and buried in trying to figure out how to carry out his plans. She reminded me that God had my future under control and would continue to lead me step by step. She emphasized that I simply needed to trust him, listen for his voice within me, and follow him.

My greatest attendant—my Naomi—was my mother, Ismona Durogene. She gave me the greatest instruction in life, some of which began before my birth.

In 1981 she fled her Caribbean country, Borgne, Haiti, by wooden raft to Miami, Florida, with the vision that her future children would experience a life far different from and better than she had as a child raised in a Third World country. Though Haiti is a gorgeous island known for its beauty as the Pearl of the Antilles, it lacked the resources my mother desired for her future and her children. Through her life experiences, she taught me that when I don't have what I need, I must seek it out and reposition myself to ensure the fulfillment of my vision.

My mother provided much instruction, not only through her words but also by example. She was a dedicated mother who worked tirelessly to provide for our family. As I recall my sixth-grade year, I remember that she worked both a day job and night job, which didn't allow time for her to cook dinner. She'd rise early every morning to prepare dinner for that evening so we would be well fed. She made sure we were off to school each morning; then she'd walk to the downtown bus terminal to begin her workday as a maid for a hotel. Once we had returned home from school, she would arrive and warm the dinner she'd prepared that morning, then change her clothes and go to her evening job, cleaning at the university.

Work ethic was an essential instruction my mother taught and exampled to me. She'd say, "If you want more, you have to work hard." She was a diligent worker who never complained about her duties, and she was grateful for all God had given her and enabled her to do.

My mom is the oldest girl of nine children. Her dad died when she was only eleven. She had to leave her schooling to work in the sugarcane fields with her mother to help support their large family. Consequently, she gained only a sixth-grade education. Yet God, in his grace, mercy, and love, had gifted her with wisdom and knowledge beyond her formal education. She worked to pass these gifts to her children. She stressed the importance of formal education, knowing a good education would enable us to have better lives than she had been able to provide as a single parent working two manually intensive jobs.

She also instructed and demonstrated the importance of a relationship with God through her lifestyle of prayer and gratitude to him. Nightly, she got down on her knees—after an extremely long day juggling two jobs, four children, and a home—and said, "Thank you, Lord." The memories of my mother kneeling in prayer are painted vividly in my mind. She taught me to always revere the Lord and give thanks—in both good times and bad.

Give thanks in all circumstances;
for this is God's will for you in Christ Jesus.
1 Thessalonians 5:18

My mother's prayers have traveled well beyond her imagination and hard work. Her faith in God has not returned void. Although my siblings and I grew up in what some call "the ghetto," my brothers avoided the penal system, and my sister and I beat the odds by not becoming statistical teenage mothers.

By example, my mother proved to us that God is in the business of multiplying whatever he has given us when we choose to invest it wisely, as demonstrated in the parable of the bags of gold in Matthew 25:14–30. She also proved Isaiah 55:11—God's Word will not return void. She saw two of her children earn college degrees and one continue on to obtain a master's degree. Though we have each experienced many dry seasons, God has always been in the midst of our family's journey and has always provided.

To him who is able to do immeasurably
more than all we ask or imagine, according to his
power that is at work within us, to him be glory ...
in Christ Jesus throughout all generations,
for ever and ever! Amen.
Ephesians 3:20–21

The Spirit-led instruction of these five attendants has been a sturdy ship for me, carrying me further into my divine destination and saving me whenever I felt as though I was drowning. Each of these five mentors have played an important role in my life that has reaffirmed for me, again and again, that *it's okay to be single* because I know who I am as a woman of God and as his child. I know he has a great plan for my life. It continues to magnificently unfold and keeps me in amazement and awe of him.

Chapter 7
The Season of Singleness

To every thing there is a season,
and a time to every purpose under the heaven.
Ecclesiastes 3:1 KJV

I needed a season of singleness to remove sinful things from my life and allow God to prepare me to be a godly wife. A key part of this preparation was falling in love with my Savior, Jesus, before falling in love with a man. Another part of the preparation was to fall in love with the woman I saw in the mirror each morning. Without true love for God and for myself as his creation prior to marriage, my future husband would be challenged in his efforts to fulfill God's command to love me "as Christ loved the church" (Ephesians 5:25 ESV).

I needed a season of singleness to heal from the deep pain of broken promises and to regain trust and growth by receiving, believing, and living God's promises and commands. Through the Spirit of God at work in me, I learned that I have a choice in how I respond to disappointments and to those who disappoint me. I can choose to respond with the same love, grace, mercy, forgiveness, and countless second chances God extends to me each day, or I can choose to respond through my human, sinful nature that blocks God's light from shining through me.

Let your light shine before others,
that they may see your good deeds
and glorify your Father in heaven.
Matthew 5:16

Through my season of singleness, I became content, knowing the day would come when my Mr. Right would walk into my life and ask for my hand in marriage. I call him "Mr. Right" because by God's design he will be right for me and will love me right: "Husbands, love your wives, just as Christ loved the church and gave himself up for her" (Ephesians 5:25). Likewise, I will be right for him because I have submitted to God's loving preparation process to become the kind of wife God desires: "Wives, submit yourselves to your own husbands as you do to the Lord" (Ephesians 5:22).

Before my season of singleness, I would not have been a Proverbs 31 wife—a wife of noble character. I would not have been ready and willing to submit to God's order of authority for marriage. Just as two cannot effectively lead in a couple's dance, two cannot effectively lead in the marriage relationship. Tragically, the world has a skewed perception of God's design for the marriage relationship. The truth is, if a husband loves his wife as Christ loved the church, his wife will be eager to allow him to lead in their relationship, and both will be fulfilled and contented in that *partnership*. God will hold every husband accountable for the way he loves his wife and leads in their relationship. He will also hold every wife accountable for how she responds to her husband's leadership.

In my season of singleness, I'm developing new strength and direction. Just as Esther's purification process made her stronger of mind and spirit, my purification process strengthened me. Today, I stand as a stronger woman of God, ready for his purposes and for my future mate in God's perfect time.

In my twenty-eighth year I attended a wedding every month. Just as steadily, family and friends continued to ask me the same questions: "When are you going to get married? When are you going to settle down and have kids?" Years ago, the "when" questions hit me hard because I didn't understand that a season of singleness was God's best for me. I'm no longer affected by the questions, comments, and opinions of others because I now understand my position in God's kingdom. I also realize that people often lack understanding of God's purposes for me and of my joy and contentment with Christ as a single woman. With each comment or question about my single status, I can honestly smile because I'm confident I will one day marry and confident that he will be God's exceptional man for me. While others are concerned about when I will wear my white dress and have children, I'm reminded that God is the author and finisher of my faith and has clothed me in the white gown of his righteousness. And I remember this promise: "I know the plans I have for you … plans to prosper you and not to harm you, plans to give you hope and a future" (Jeremiah 29:11).

I'm not only happy and contented in singleness but also love where I am as a single woman. I embrace with confidence the truth that *it's okay to be single* because in singleness I've learned who God created me to be. This season of singleness has also given me the gift of time to discern what I really desire in a mate.

Put simply, singleness is a *priceless place of preparation*. It's God's gift of time for singles to grow spiritually and emotionally and to establish a solid foundation of faith in Christ, the Rock.

Chapter 8

Contentment

*Seek first the kingdom of God and his righteousness,
and all these things will be added to you.*
Matthew 6:33 ESV

Why is it okay to be single? Because God has everything already worked out for our good and because life is already happening all around us! Life doesn't begin at the wedding altar. Life is right now. There's no need to force a relationship but every need to be content and patient while waiting for a mate.

I consider how social media and reality television perpetuates the enemy's lie that something must be wrong if an individual is not in a relationship or doesn't have a ring and a date set by their late twenties. Societal expectations often create anxiety and desperation in the single person when, in truth, it's either not yet God's perfect time for a relationship that will honor him and be fulfilling or it's not yet the right person.

Once desperation occupies the heart and mind, it quickly evolves into the mentality that one must find a mate by any means possible. What could be an amazing journey with Jesus toward readiness for marriage sadly becomes The Great Race for a mate, cheered on by the crowd toward the finish line—the altar. Tragically, many in the cheering crowd are unhappily married individuals. I say "individuals" rather than "couples" because they have not yet coupled as *one* with each other as God intended.

When I've posted a picture of myself attending someone's wedding, the comments in response have often attested to that cheering crowd. When I turned from desperation, by giving myself fully to Christ, those comments no longer bothered me. Attending the weddings of family and friends, I can smile with genuine joy and contentment because I'm confident my time will come and it will be right.

It's my wish that all singles around the world will put off anxiety, panic, and desperation and embrace contentment with Christ. Single men and women who are desperate to be validated by a relationship too often marry the first person they can, deceived (by lack of knowing their worth in Christ) into prematurely walking down the aisle. I have attended a number of weddings where the love was genuine and it was clear God had orchestrated the union. I have also attended weddings where it was clear that the two were forcing a love relationship. A forced relationship will not endure the test of time and trials.

Too often I have seen relationships develop into marriage between two people who are not assigned by their Creator to become one flesh. The wedding is beautiful and the food is tasty, but the union is wrong because it's either not God's divinely purposed union or not his perfect timing.

Some stand at the altar not realizing they're making a mistake. Others know in their hearts they should not walk down that aisle and take those holy vows. Yet the invitations have been sent, the dresses are bought, the limo is ready, and the reception hall is decorated.

Destiny and *purpose* are two words that come to my mind when I think of a marriage that is right because God has ordained the union and timing. How often do we see couples who have celebrated thirty, forty, and fifty years of marriage but treat each other like cell mates serving a life sentence, chained together by neediness, fear, power, religion, or money? How often do we see couples separating and divorcing after ten, twenty, thirty, or even fifty years of marriage? In contrast, how often do we see a couple living as one flesh in an authentic, Christ-centered, covenant marriage of unconditional love, respect, honor, virtue, and sacrificial giving?

Two individuals who are right for each other by God's design will share the same spiritual beliefs and the same values and ethics. They will walk together toward the same life goal. They will share a steadfast commitment to Christ and to their sacred marriage vows. They will go through life's highs and lows as one flesh, "until death do us part."

Chapter 9
Reflection

No eye has seen, no ear has heard,
and no mind has imagined the things that God
has prepared for those who love him.
1 Corinthians 2:9 ISV

Ralph Waldo Emerson said, "Life is a journey, not a destination." In reflection, I realized I had begun my young adulthood with my own destination in sight. Like many young women, I was focused on my desire to marry and live a fairytale life rather than first centering on becoming a woman of God and gaining his everlasting inheritance for me. The situations that negatively impacted my life didn't change, but God used those to show me I needed his love and guidance over my need for others.

Through my journey of singleness with him, I understand that nothing is wrong with me if I'm not married. I can live a contented, full, and fulfilling life in singleness. Had I married earlier, I would not have been a good wife because of all the issues lingering in me.

Through the years, I've read and studied the Proverbs 31 woman. That passage is the epitome of a woman of noble character. As I reflected on the lifestyle I was leading in my early twenties, certain portions of that passage really drew my attention.

Who can find a virtuous and capable wife?
She is more precious than rubies.
Her husband can trust her,
and she will greatly enrich his life.
She brings him good, not harm, all the days of her life.
Proverbs 31:10–12 NLT

At one point, still carrying all those unresolved issues, I asked myself if I was a Proverbs 31 woman. Had I been married at the time, I would not have been able to honestly say I wouldn't bring hurt to a husband. And because of the secrets I carried about my past, I would not have been able to promise him that he could trust me. Before I could become a virtuous wife—a woman of noble character, ready for a man of noble character—I had to be transformed. That transformation began with my honesty about my past and the choices I was making as an adult. I had to acknowledge that I needed help from God and from those he had placed in my life to teach and mentor me. Once I acknowledged to God my need for his help, he immediately opened his arms and embraced me—just as I was. He sat with me amidst the shambles of my life and comforted me, just as I had imagined an earthly dad would have comforted me as a child.

I prayed, devoured the Bible, and followed the wisdom of my mentors. I also sought professional help from a licensed Christian counselor. None of my family and friends knew I was seeing a counselor; I didn't tell them, because I was afraid they'd view me in a negative way—as though I weren't strong enough or smart enough to manage life issues on my own. The truth is, none of us can manage life on our own. We need not only the empowering Spirit of God but also each other. He created us to be in relationships that include and honor him and encourage us to grow spiritually and emotionally.

The heaviness of my past began to ease when I confessed to God and a human being how I had been sinned against as a child and as a young adult and how I had sinned against God and others. Once truth was released, I realized my reactions to painful memories were different. I no longer felt anger or sadness. The more I released the secret things from my heart, the more my body and spirit literally began to relax, and I began to let down my guard. I felt a freedom of heart and mind I had never before experienced, as if I had been released from a twenty-six-year prison cell. I realized I was finally *free* to be the person God had originally created me to be and free to go wherever he was leading.

CB   BD

In April 2014, I heard the Holy Spirit whisper to me, "Write." Just as I had shared my dark past and purification journey with my counselor, I sat down and began to write my truths on paper. In doing so, I realized God wanted to show me more clearly how my heart and life had changed … how I had been delivered and transformed … how my years of prayers had been answered … how I had found contentment and joy as I waited for my mate … and, most important, how he had been there for me all along as a true daddy.

My intention for this book was not to begin a singles movement nor to push people into living all their lives without marrying. This book is intended to speak encouragement and hope to single women and men who are discontented and to those who are anxiously pursuing the opposite sex for the wrong reasons—pleasure, pressure from the world, loneliness, neediness …

What I've come to know for certain is this: *It's very okay to be single.* True happiness and contentment in singleness can be found in God through Jesus Christ alone. He will meet all your needs as you wait for your mate.

After I began to walk with Christ, Deuteronomy 31:6 helped to heal me and transform my thinking: "Be strong and courageous. Do not be afraid or terrified because of them, for the LORD your God goes with you; he will never leave you nor forsake you." Reading this scripture shifted something in my spirit and I knew the disappointment and pain of broken promises were part of the enemy's plan to destroy the woman God had created me to be. Receiving and choosing to believe God's promises filled me with enormous comfort, peace, and assurance. I knew my salvation, in every regard, had come from God alone, who is greater than the enemy of my soul.

You, dear children, are from God and
have overcome them,
because the one who is in you is greater
than the one who is in the world.
1 John 4:4

Knowing that God had promised to always be present with me, through all of life's disappointments and tragedies, empowered me to be an overcomer. Being an overcomer carries many amazing promises from God. (Read 1 John 5:5; Revelation 2:26; 3:5, 21; 21:7.)

I didn't write this book to boast the delights of singleness. Like many singles, I desire to one day be married. I wrote this book to empower and encourage other singles in the truth that you can be content as you wait for your mate. Begin with honesty about your past and present life and about your choices and your relationship with Christ. Then contentment will come.

God has used everything I went through as a child and every experience of my adult life to bring me to Jesus, the Rock of my salvation. Smiling with absolute contentment, I understand that God has ordered my steps for his great purposes and I can trust him. When

I became whole through Christ, I became God's willing instrument to lead others to his saving grace and eternal riches.

It's okay to be single.

⚘ ⚘

Perhaps as you read this book, you're dealing with the emptiness of growing up in the murky shadows or in the complete darkness of an absentee parent. Perhaps you're dealing with sins committed against you or sins you've committed. Know that God is the only source of everlasting light, and he can fill your emptiness with contentment, true love, joy, and peace. He does this through his son, Jesus Christ, and through his indwelling, empowering Holy Spirit. All you need to do is be truthful with God and accept his gift of salvation. "For in him we live and move and have our being" (Acts 17:28).

My hope and prayer is that God will use my honesty to save a young woman or man from losing their purity, to save a young woman from becoming pregnant and suffering a miscarriage or unwanted pregnancy, and to save an individual from marrying the wrong person or marrying before it's the right time.

If one reader decides to follow Christ, waiting patiently and contentedly for God's best in a mate, my assignment is fulfilled. Why settle for less when you can have your Creator's best?

If you're single, or if you're one among the cheering crowd of married people who are pushing singles toward the marriage altar, my hope and prayer is that you better understand through my story why it's so very okay to be single.

The quiet times that come with being single are the very moments when one can learn to keenly hear God speaking. A communion of conversation with your heavenly Daddy, Abba, is similar to our communication with one another. All relationships begin with conversation, and a deepening relationship requires regular, ongoing communication. Your heavenly Father is right there with you now, eager to listen to you and just as eager to talk with you. He's eager to show you that he is wholly faithful, dependable, powerful, and empowering. He's eager to fill you with his incomprehensible love, grace, mercy, peace, joy, kindness, gentleness, goodness, and self-control. These are some of his characteristics and the fruit of his Spirit.

Communicating with him daily comes in two distinctive forms: prayer and reading his Word. In this heavenly relationship, like none other, you will find contentment. He's also the most creative date you will ever have! Adventures with Christ will leave you breathless with awe.

Your season of singleness is a gift of time from your heavenly Daddy in which you can become transformed and truly prepared for the next phase of your life. It's also the gift of time to accomplish the special assignments he's already placed before you "for such a time as this" (Esther 4:14).

Will you choose to give yourself fully to God and step out in faith to follow him? Will you embrace your singleness in a journey with his son, Jesus Christ? If you love and follow God, he promises to work *all* things in your life for your good. Will you trust him?

Fall in love with your heavenly Father first. Love him above all others and above all things, and you will reap all the riches of his kingdom as you wait for your mate.

Take delight in the LORD,
and he will give you the desires of your heart.
Psalm 37:4

About the Author

LAURANE SIMON is a graduate of the notable Florida Agriculture & Mechanical University of Tallahassee, Florida. In this debut book, she shares her personal life experiences which lead her to a place of solitude in her single status. She is not projecting a singles movement, but is encouraging men and women to embrace their relationship status. She writes to the reader with the intentions that a single woman or man would read the book and understand that singleness is not a death sentence, but an opportunity to get oneself in alignment to prepare for a life mate. She currently lives in Fort Lauderdale, Florida.

www.ingramcontent.com/pod-product-compliance
Lightning Source LLC
Chambersburg PA
CBHW060611030426
42337CB00018B/3042